for Attitude

Written and Illustrated by Julie Davey

A for Attitude Productions
www.aforattitude.com.au

Text and Illustrations copyright © Julie Davey, 2003

First published in Australia by Hen & Ink Productions 1998 ISBN 0-646-35657-7
Bantam edition 1999 ISBN 1-86325-206-1
Times Editions Singapore edition 2002 ISBN 981-232-481-X

Fourth edition published in Australia and New Zealand 2003

A for Attitude Productions
PO Box 33 McCrae
Victoria 3938 Australia

http://www.aforattitude.com.au
e-mail: info@aforattitude.com.au

Printed in Australia by Sands Print Group.

National Library of Australia
Cataloguing-in-Publication entry:

     Davey, Julie.
     A for attitude : a little book of inspiration and encouragement.

     Includes index.
     ISBN 0 9750698 0 2.

     1. Self-actualization (Psychology).
     2. Attitude (Psychology). I. Title.

    158.1

for
Scott, Stephen and Tom

Thank you to all those people who
have given me their support, encouragement
and valuable feedback during the production of this book…

Yvonne Davey,
Louise Corben,
Tracey Courtney,
Jan O'Connell,
Dr Estelle Morrison

and

Raymond F. Smith
a friend and mentor
who has very generously shared his time
and artistic knowledge over the years.

Special thanks to Tracey and Trevor Courtney
of Tranceformations
for helping me to find my true porpoise.

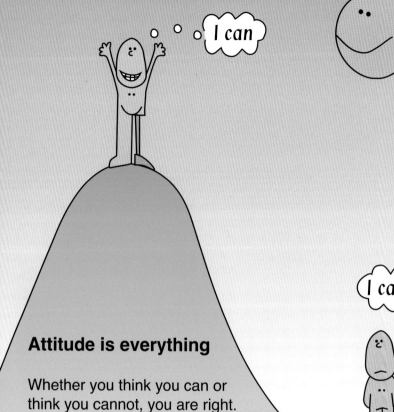

Attitude is everything

Whether you think you can or
think you cannot, you are right.
— Henry Ford said that.

One of the few things in life that
we have total control over is our attitude.

Notice how much easier it is
to get things done when you decide to try.

Achievement

…what happens when we **plan**
for something and work at it until it **happens**.

You can give yourself a 'pat on the back' every time
you achieve something you have worked for.

Think of things that you have
achieved so far in your life.

Remember the good feeling
you had when you first got
your shoes on the **right** feet,

– or read a book **on your own**.

Write down all
the things you
can do well.

Make a list of
things you would
like to do.

Work on your
'like to do' list until you
achieve those things.

Admit when you are wrong

There is no-one in the world
who is always right.

If you think
you are always right,
you will never learn
from your mistakes.

If you make a mistake,

see
what
you
can
learn
from
it.

Be willing to apologise.

It often makes
the other person
and you
feel much better.

Affirmations

are things we say to ourselves
about what we want to do
or what we would like to have.

Write down your affirmations and
then say them aloud, in private,
as often as you can.

By affirming that you can
achieve your goal,
you will find yourself succeeding.

On the other hand,
if you say you can't do it
then you most certainly won't!

Animals

Be kind to animals.
They have the right to live happily
and safely in this world.

So put yourself in their place.
Imagine that the animals rule the world and
that some people live in zoos while others are
kept by the animals as pets.

The animals are responsible for the
care of their 'pet' humans, so you
have to wait until the frogs
come home from soccer
practice before
you get fed at night.
**You know frogs,
they stay out all night!**

And for your exercise,
you have to wait for the cats to
stop watching TV to take you for a walk.

If you have a pet at home,
remember to give it plenty of love and attention,
because your pet gives you so much.

Anger

We all feel angry at times,
and it is important to get rid of our anger
without hurting ourselves or others.

1   Get away from the thing
that is making you angry.
When you do, it is usually
easier to deal with the problem
and think more clearly.

2   Exercise is a great way of letting it out.
Kick a football,
run around the block,

hit a tennis ball,
go for a walk,
yell into your pillow.

Remember that if you do or say something
when you are angry, you can't take it back.

If someone has treated you unfairly,
it may be nothing to do with you.

Don't let it become your problem.

Balance

work and play,
rest and activity.

We all need time
to play games.
But what would
happen if we
played
all the time?

Nothing
would get done,
we wouldn't learn
new skills.

If we had
sunshine
all the time,
without rain,
the plants
would not
grow.

And if we worked
without playing,
we would be very
dull people.

We need to keep a balance of things in our life.

Think of some things that have
opposites to balance them.

happy   *sad*

old   *new*

14.

Believe in yourself

… no matter what other people think of you.

Decide that you can do, be and have
whatever you want in this world
and the only person
who
can
get
you
there
... is
YOU

Best

Do the best you can with your natural gifts –
that is all you have to do.

You don't have to be **the** best,
but it is important to
be **your** best.

Boomerangs

Your thoughts are boomerangs.

In helping others you help yourself.
In hurting others, you hurt yourself.
It may not happen today or tomorrow,
but sooner or later the thoughts you put out
come back to you – good and not-so-good.

Choose to be good to yourself!

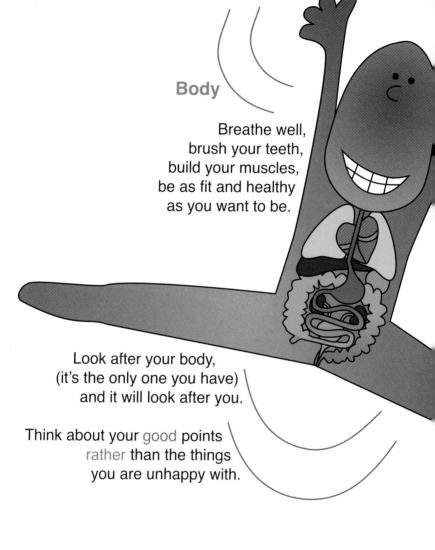

Body

Breathe well,
brush your teeth,
build your muscles,
be as fit and healthy
as you want to be.

Look after your body,
(it's the only one you have)
and it will look after you.

Think about your good points
rather than the things
you are unhappy with.

Bullies

These are people who have problems within **themselves.**

They are usually unhappy and so they decide to hurt others.

People who are happy in themselves have no need to hurt others.

Choices

You can **choose** to think
and behave in certain ways that help you
to be a happier and more successful person.

You can **choose** to
think positive thoughts
about yourself
and you can **choose**
to be friendly and helpful
to others.

You can **choose** your friends.

You can **choose** to try.

You can **choose** to follow everyone else,
or you can **choose** to do what is right for you.

Who you are
is a result of the choices you make.

Complaining

Think about whether the thing is
worth complaining about.
Is it unjust?
If it is, then see if
you can change it.

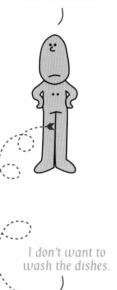

*I don't want to
wash the dishes.*

*I don't want to
wash the dishes.*

If you grumble about
something that you
don't want to do,
but know
is really necessary,
then you are just
making yourself
miserable
for nothing.

In the end
you still
have to do
the thing.

It takes
time away
from doing
the things
you really
want to do.

*I don't want to
wash the dishes,
but I do like to
use clean dishes.*

later...

Creativity

…comes from using your imagination.

Each one of us is creative
in one way or another.

How are **you** creative?

Write your **own story,**
or finish this one, and then maybe
draw a picture about your story.
Have a go. Have fun!

Once upon a time, there was a funny old ferret called
Racey McStroodlehuff who lived in a very
fancy tunnel.

One day while he was busy digging
an extension (for a guest room),
he heard a loud "woop woop sproing"
noise outside.

When Racey went to see what
was going on, he couldn't
believe his eyes.

There, right in the middle of the path was a huge, red...

Dare to be different

The people who make a big difference in this world
are usually doing something **different** from everyone else.

Because of this we have computers, bubblegum,
life-saving medicines, rock-and-roll music, in-line skates,
modern art, blue jeans and pizzas.

Your ideas are important.
Think your own thoughts and be yourself.
You might come up with something that
will make the world a better place.

If you accept things as they are, that is all you will ever know.

Dare to dream of how you would like things to be.
Dream it. Plan it. Do it.

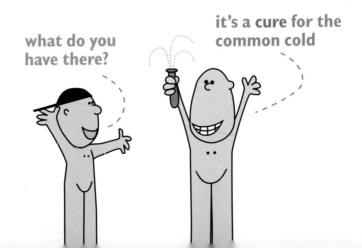

Decide to be...

• **happy** – see if you can do it!
When you wake up each morning
decide that it will
be a good day.

• **healthy**
– Decide to eat more fruit
and vegetables,
exercise more,
breathe deeply.

• **successful** –
This doesn't
mean you have
to be the best at
everything,
– there are many
kinds of success.

If you are running a
marathon
you may not win the race,
but if you finish the course,
you are still successful.

Decide to be...whatever you want to be.

Energy

...positive
or
negative –
what we give out
affects others.

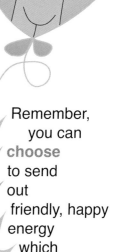

Do you
like
to be
around
grumpy
people?

Notice
how
their
energy
affects
you?

Remember,
you can
choose
to send
out
friendly, happy
energy
which
then
attracts
friendly, happy
people
to you.

Give it a go and
see how it feels.

Enough

You are enough.

You have all of the
talent, strength and ability
you need to succeed in this world.

Understand what you have
and focus on these things,
not what you **think** is missing.

Expectations

Live up to
your expectations of yourself,
not other people's.

Faith in your ability

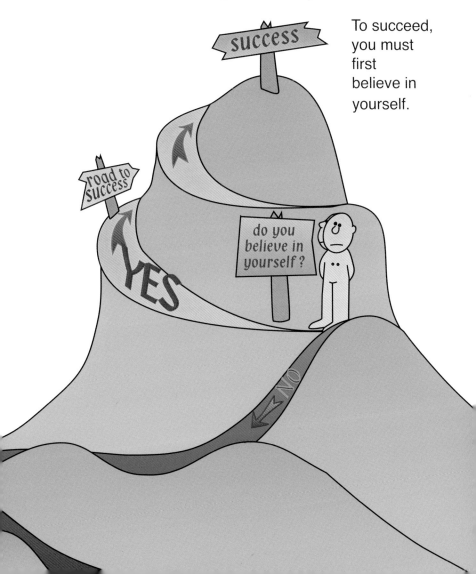

To succeed, you must first believe in yourself.

Fear is our worst enemy

Sometimes by worrying,
you actually attract trouble.

Fear of what might happen,
is a waste of time and energy.

If the thing you are worrying about doesn't happen,
you have wasted all that time for nothing.

Think about the thing you fear.
Now think about the worst thing that **could** happen.
Is it really **likely** to happen?
Is there something you could
learn from it if it does happen?

Think about things you have feared in the past,
and how you feel about them now.

Fear can stop you trying new things.

The best way to overcome fear is
to imagine in your mind
a picture of yourself handling the problem
with great confidence.

If you have a fear of heights...

imagine yourself doing these things
step by step, taking your time, until
you are ready to move on –

1 you are happily standing on a chair
2 you are standing halfway up a ladder and smiling
3 wow, you are standing on a balcony and laughing
4 look at you now, you are walking across a footbridge
5 now picture something
   really big…

You could try saying
"I am happily standing
on top of Uluru.
I feel secure."

This way,
you **see a picture**
in your mind of
a happy, secure person.

Feelings affect your body

Some people can heal themselves
by **deciding** that they will get better.

You can also talk yourself into getting sick.

If you tell yourself that
you will catch that cold,
you are likely to.

Choose to be well.

when you love someone,
you feel warm...
you smile and laugh...
you feel full of energy...

when you are afraid,
your heart thumps...
you sweat...
your knees knock...
sometimes you cry...

Fun

Fun is a very important part of life –
just as long as you play safely.

When you are doing something
you enjoy, your body releases
natural chemicals called
'endorphins' into your
blood stream.

These are
good
for you.

They help you to
stay well and to
look and feel
better.

Go for it,
have fun!

Give

When you give to others,
you are really giving to yourself.

Have you noticed the
warm feeling you get when
you give away something,
and the other person is pleased?

You have made two people happy.

Goals

These are things you would like to achieve.

They can be about what you
want to achieve this week, this year
or this century.

Examples: getting fitter,
playing your sport better,
getting over an illness,
seeing different places,
meeting different people,
learning new skills,
feeling happier, and much more...

If you ask **successful** people
how they made it to the top,
they will probably tell you
that they saw a picture of themselves
being successful –
first in their mind,
and then they **worked** towards the day
when everyone else would
see the same picture.

- Begin with something small, that you can achieve soon.

- Make the goal **personal**, for you alone, (and nothing to do with anyone else).

- Be **realistic**.
  Focus on things that are possible to achieve.

- Be **exact** in what you aim for. Perhaps you would like to score more points in basketball.

- Decide **when** you will score 2, 4 or 10 points in a game – by Christmas, or by next July...

- Write these details down and look at them often.
  Tell yourself that you will achieve them.

More about setting Goals

Write an affirmation about you achieving your goal.

e.g. **I am happily…**

- **See** yourself throwing the ball through the hoop!

- Imagine the score sheet with the points scored next to your name.

- **Believe** that you can and will improve your point scoring.

- Draw a picture of **you** scoring points and perhaps put it on your wardrobe door, look at it **often**.

- Think about how you can achieve your goal and who can help you… (maybe your coach, or a friend who can **practise** with you)

- Then work on ways of achieving this goal... e.g. work at it, practise, practise, practise...

  Draw a picture here of yourself practising

- If you want to tell other people about your goals, make sure they are people who would be happy to see you win.

- When you are confident with your goal setting, move on to more challenging targets.

Gossip

Before you spread gossip
about someone,
stop and think
how you
would feel
if people were
talking about you
behind
your back.

Would you like your
secrets spread
around school?

Is the gossip even true?

Could it make
the other person sad?
Could it make them lose friends?

Starting today, you can choose to
be a loving friendly person, or a nosy parker.

It's up to you.

Health

Body and Mind

Growing bodies need to be fed good, fresh food
to help them to work properly.

Activity is also important for a healthy body
and a healthy mind.

Did you ever notice how happy you feel
after exercise or play?

That's your body letting you
know it likes to be active.

At other times your body
might give you a
headache when
you feed it
too many sweets.

Our bodies give us
messages
all the time about
what is best for us.

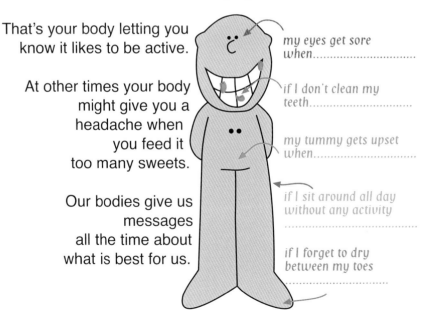

my eyes get sore
when.............................

if I don't clean my
teeth..............................

my tummy gets upset
when.............................

if I sit around all day
without any activity
....

if I forget to dry
between my toes
....

Honesty

It may not matter to you
now
what people think of you,
but when it comes to getting a job,
or being able to do something
you really want to do
later on it will matter how you have
chosen to live your life.

Telling lies brings you trouble.

Do you want people to be able to trust you?

Imagination

What we see in our minds can become real for us…

This is where we dream up and plan our futures.
And also where we let our minds run free
just for the fun of it.

What will I wear to the party?

What will I do when I grow up?

What if we could fly like birds?

What would it be like to walk in space?

Immune system

This is the way your body
fights diseases for you.

It is like the guards
surrounding the castle,
defending you from the invaders!

To keep it working well,
you need to have a
positive (happy) attitude
about yourself and your body,
plenty of activity and a healthy diet.

Try to look on the bright side of life.
When things happen that
you **think** are against you,
look a bit closer and see if there is
some **good** in this thing.

Feelings like worry
and anger can weaken
your immune system, and
make you sick.

**Notice how well you feel
when you are happy.**

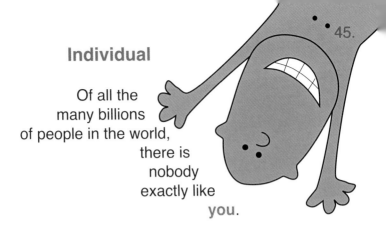

Individual

Of all the
many billions
of people in the world,
there is
nobody
exactly like
you.

We all have our **own** talents and abilities.

It would be very boring if we were all the same.

Just think, we might have
plenty of doctors but no nurses,
or if everyone wanted to be an actor,
who would work the cameras,
develop the film and
sell the tickets at the theatre?

If everyone worked in an office,
who would grow our food
and remove our rubbish?

Be proud of what you do well.

Intuition

Some people call this your 'gut' feeling, because it comes from inside you.

This can warn you of danger or things to be careful of.

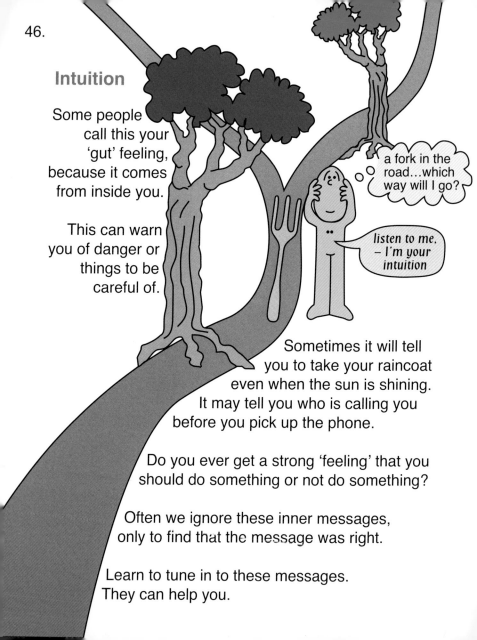

a fork in the road...which way will I go?

listen to me, — I'm your intuition

Sometimes it will tell you to take your raincoat even when the sun is shining. It may tell you who is calling you before you pick up the phone.

Do you ever get a strong 'feeling' that you should do something or not do something?

Often we ignore these inner messages, only to find that the message was right.

Learn to tune in to these messages. They can help you.

Jealousy

Being jealous of others is
a waste of time and energy.

It gets you nowhere and makes you unhappy.

Be happy for the good fortune of others
and concentrate on
your own good points or strengths.

48.

Laughter

Some people
say
that
laughter
is
the
best
medicine.

There is a hospital
in the USA
that shows its patients
funny movies each day
as part of their treatment.
This helps them to get better.

Laugh every day
and see how good it feels!

Lessons

We all have
lessons to learn in life,
no matter how old we are.

People around you and
things that happen to you
can show you something
you can learn.

Look out for your lessons.

If you learn from things that happen in your life,
you will find that things will be easier for you.

Just as if you continually find
yourself in trouble, it is because
you are not learning
these lessons.

That's the third time this week!

I'd better make a note to avoid the thin branches after a big lunch...

Like attracts like

You attract people to you who behave the way you do.

Look

Look for the good in others, and that is what you will find.

What you **focus on**, **increases**.

If you look out for yellow cars on the road you will be surprised at how many there are. They were always there, you probably just didn't see them.

It is the same with **people** – they all have good qualities. You just need to **look** for them.

Mind

What you
put into your mind is
what will **come out** of it.

If you read gloomy stories and listen to gossip,
guess what will be filling your mind?

Do you want to be
happy and positive?

If so, concentrate on positive stories
and listen to positive people.

Remember, what you focus on, grows.

Meditation

Time out to relax your mind and body.

Here is a basic meditation you can try.

1   Find a **quiet** spot where you won't be disturbed.

2   Close your eyes and think about your breathing.

3   Take slow deep breaths in and out and **picture** yourself in a beautiful forest beside a sparkling stream full of **splashing gold fish**

4   Look around your **forest** and see how many baby animals you can notice. What kind of animals are they? How many can you see?

5   Imagine that one animal comes up to you for a cuddle and a play. How do you **feel**?
    Stay for a while and play with your new friend.

6   When you are ready, imagine leaving the forest and come back to the room that you are in.

How do you feel now?

Mistakes

The person who makes no mistakes,
does not usually make anything.

— Edward John Phelps said that.

Learn from your mistakes and
try again in a different way.

Thomas Edison invented the light bulb.
It took him thousands of attempts before he got it right.

The greatest mistake you can make
is to be afraid of making one.
You only fail when you stop trying.

Name calling

**Sticks and stones
may break my bones
but names will
never hurt me.**
– This is an old proverb.

You decide how you feel inside, **you** decide whether
to let other people's opinions hurt you.

Choose to be confident and know you are okay.
You can do it.

Pretend that you are confident
until it comes naturally.

NOW

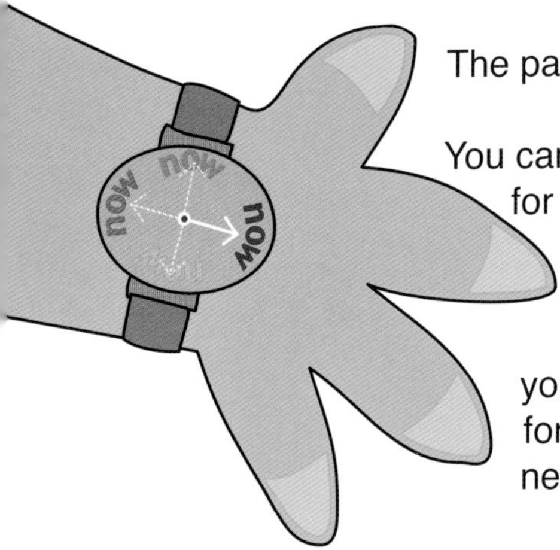

Live in the present moment.

The past is gone.

You can plan
for the future,
but if you are
always living
for tomorrow,
you will never get there,
for tomorrow
never comes.

**Now is the only moment that really matters.
Enjoy each moment.**

Opinions

If you judge yourself **only** on what others think of you,
you will never be happy, because
there will always be people with **different** ideas to you.
You will be making them more important than you.

What other people say about or to you can only affect
you if you believe what they say is true.
You are in charge of how you feel.

**No-one can make you feel inferior
without your consent.**
– Eleanor Roosevelt said that.

Some people offer their opinions as advice.
This can be helpful, and is worth thinking about.
However, in the end, it is your decision to do
what feels right
for you.

Opportunities

In the middle of difficulty,
you will find an opportunity.

Opportunities are always there –
we just need to look for them.

Every cloud has a silver lining.
— This is an old proverb.

Persistence

If you truly want to achieve something,
and if you truly believe you can do it,
keep at it.

keep going,
you can do it!

Anything worth having
is worth working for.

Every step you take is a step closer to
achieving your goal.

nearly
there

You may be
clever enough,
strong enough
and talented enough;
however without persistence,
these
qualities
are not
enough.

60.

Problems

…are great opportunities to learn and grow.

Everyone has problems,
and all problems have
solutions.

You can sort some problems out
yourself or you may need to
ask someone
to help
you.

We all need help
sometimes.

Prejudices

Means to pre-judge –
to decide something before you have all the facts.
Sometimes we decide things about people
just by looking at them, or hearing their voices.

Did you ever get a big beautifully wrapped present for your
birthday, and decided you **knew** what was in the box before
you tore off the wrapping paper, only to find when you opened
it up, that it wasn't what you were expecting after all?

You were pre-judging.

It's the same with people.
Just because they look or sound different
(we all do anyway)
it doesn't mean that they should be treated
any differently.

Remember it is how you **act** that is important.

Happiness is finding your life's porpoise

Purpose

**Live your life on "porpoise".
We are all different, and have
different skills and talents.**

**When you find something that makes you feel good
inside, without hurting others, then focus on this thing
– you might be happily surprised where it leads you.**

Quit

There are habits that we have
that are not helping us,
and it's great to be able to quit these.

What are some of the habits you have,
that you would like to quit?

By **writing them down** and affirming that you
want to quit your habits,
you are on your way.

Rejoice
in who you are

Be proud of yourself – you are unique.

Rejection

If someone won't be your friend,
it may be nothing to do with you at all.
It may be their problem, not yours.

Is there anyone you know of in this world,
who is liked by everyone?

We cannot control how other people think.
We cannot expect everyone to like us.
There are billions of people in this world.
Find the ones who do want to be your friends.

You need to be happy with yourself first and then
you will find that other people want to be with you.

I only make friends
with people
who have a 'Q' in
their names…

*Well, that's a shame
because we were just about
to ask you to come to the
movies with us.*

Relaxation

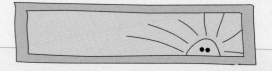

Read a book.

Go for a walk.

Pat a cat.

Cuddle a teddy bear.

Have a bath.

Try some meditation.

Responsibility

...for yourself

We are all responsible for our actions and our future.

Whether you want to be a rocket scientist
or a rock star, you will need to put in the work.

It doesn't matter what other people around you are doing,
you are responsible for what you do.

You can't blame
anyone else for
the choices you make.

If you are doing something
you know is wrong just
because your friends
are telling you to,
then you are fooling yourself.

Are you coming
out to play?

After I have
finished my
homework –
I'll be there.

...for others

If you run through a crowded place and knock
someone over and hurt them,
you are responsible for that also.

...for animals

If you choose to have a pet, then it is your responsibility to:

- Feed it
- Give it fresh water every day
- Make sure it has plenty of exercise
- Make sure it has vaccinations from a vet every year to keep it healthy
- & Give it lots of **love.**

...for the environment

We are responsible for our environment.

Our world is being polluted by irresponsible people and it is affecting us all every day.

An unhealthy world makes us unhealthy too. Think of ways you can help.

(Read more about this under the "World" heading)

Rewards

Plant good thoughts, ideas, words, actions NOW.
Enjoy good rewards LATER.

You get out of life what you put into it.
Eventually you will be rewarded for your behaviour.

Self-acceptance

This is one of the keys to success.

Learn to love and respect yourself,
and believe that you deserve
good things in your life.
Then it will be easier to achieve your goals.

If you don't accept yourself for who you are,
how do you expect other people to?

Look in the mirror every day
and tell yourself that you
are as good
as anyone
else.

Sadness

It's OK to feel sad
sometimes.

Letting your feelings out is healthy,
as long as you let go of them in a way that
doesn't hurt anyone around you.

Have you noticed that
after you cry,
you feel better?

If you keep sadness
inside of you,
it can
make
you sick.

Self-pity

This is feeling sorry for yourself.

Think about how you can fix
whatever is making you feel sad,
rather than concentrating on the problem.

Remember – whatever you focus on, grows.

Ask for **help**, rather than **sympathy**.
Other people will be more willing to help you
if you are willing to help yourself.

Soul, Spirit

This is the thing inside us that
makes us **different** from
every other person on the earth.

Think about people who have an
identical twin – what makes them different?
...It's their spirits!

Your spirit can help you to get well after being sick
and to achieve your goals.
Your spirit makes you **special.**

Success

Doing what you set out to do.

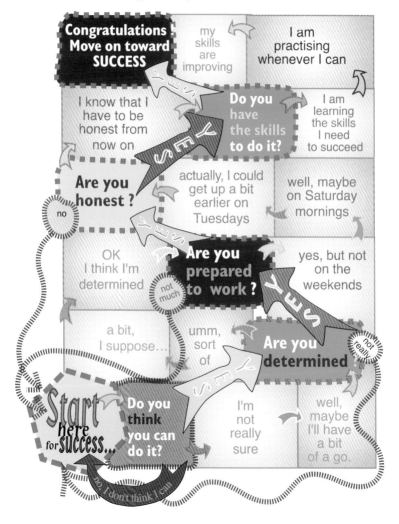

Thanks

Be thankful for
your natural gifts
and talents,
for your abilities,
for everything you are.

When you thank someone for a gift
or for doing something for you,
that is like giving them back a present.

It lets them know
they are appreciated.

Thoughts

Every thought you have had and
every deed you have done,
made you who you are today.

Think about it. Are you a positive person?
Do you think you can – or think you cannot?
You can start today to be who you want to be.

Think about the sort of person you want to be
and hold on to that thought.

If you are already happy with yourself,
then keep up the good work!

Treat other people as you
would like them to treat you

…and maybe one day they will.

Truth

Be true to yourself –

what is right for others is not always right for you.

If you do or say things that don't 'feel right' to you,
just to be popular among your friends,
then you are letting yourself down and
you may find yourself in big trouble.

Your feelings are a very good guide.
Listen to them.
Listen to your inner truth.

Real friends will be drawn to you
because of your inner strength.

You are important.

Universal energy

Every living thing has an energy field.

Some energy can be seen; however, we usually feel
the energy from most things, including people.

Which of these energy fields have you sensed?

- the sun
- the moon
- the wind
- a waterfall
- the ocean
- a candle
- someone you hugged
- a big leafy tree

How does their energy affect you?

Can you add to this list?

The universe we live in has a special energy
that you can use whenever you like.
All you need is your imagination.

Try this exercise.

Get very still – close your eyes.
Imagine you are surrounded by a field of
pure energy. It may be white
or all the colours of the rainbow. That's up to you.
Breathe in the positive, happy energy.
Breathe out your problems and negative thoughts.
Do this 4 or 5 times.
How do you feel now?

View

It is not so much what
happens to us that affects us,
more often it is the way we **view** it
and how we **let** it affect us.

For example...
You look outside to see the rain pouring down.
You were planning on going out to play.
Well, you could sit inside and sulk all day,
or you could find another fun activity to do inside –
make something, draw pictures,
read a book, invite friends over.

It's your choice.

Whatever you do or say, you will not stop the rain.
Of course, on the other hand if you are a duck,
you'll love to see it raining outside!

It's all in the way you **view** things.

World

At the moment, the world is out of balance.

We need to believe that we can heal the world.

If we each do our little bit, we will achieve much
as a group working together.

If we try, we have a chance.
If we give up and think we are lost,
then we most certainly will be.

Here are some things we can do:

- Conserve our forests.
- Clean up our parks.
- Look after the animals.
- Recycle our rubbish.
- Use less plastic.
- Think more about our actions…

and – as John Lennon said –
- "Give **peace** a chance".

Let's try to leave this world in a
better way than we found it.
It can be done…
We can make a difference.
Let's do it.

Yourself

The most important person
in your world is you.

This doesn't mean be selfish,
but it does mean not to put
everyone else before you,
all of the time.

You cannot help others if you neglect yourself.

Eat well, exercise, work and play, have fun.

The best way to get the
love and respect of other people
is to love and respect...

Yourself

Index

The Dream Tree

If you have problems that are really bothering you,
write them down on paper. This may help you to sort them out.
The tree on the back of this page
is for you to hang your thoughts upon.

1… Carefully remove this page from the book and laminate it.
2… Trace around this leaf (or design your own)
– make the leaves as large as you like
3… Write your worries on these leaves.
4… Hang them on the tree.
5… Before you go to sleep at night,
put the picture under your pillow.

When you wake up in the morning,
you may find that you have
some new ideas about how
you can sort out your worries.

You can also hang your **wishes** upon the Dream Tree!…
What good things would you like to have happen
for you, your family or your friends?
What great things would you like to see happen in the world?

Write these things down on your Dream Tree leaves
and place them on the tree, under your pillow at night.
Pleasant Dreams!

After removing the page from the book, you can preserve the picture by laminating it